PRAYERS FOR EVERYONE™
STRENGTH
(BOOK 1)

PRAYERS FOR EVERYONE™
STRENGTH
(BOOK 1)

by

Nicole Rivera

Printed in the United States of America

ISBN-10: 0692224815
ISBN-13: 978-0692224816

Isaiah Publications (New York City)
cs@isaiahpublications.com

For additional titles in the Prayers For Everyone™ series please visit http://www.nicolerivera.com.

Dedicated to seekers of the truth. May all of your desires be fulfilled and may you be uplifted to the greatness that you already are.

TABLE OF CONTENTS

Introduction	1
Definitions	5
I Pray	7
Infused	9
Embodiment	11
I Am Strength	13
I Am That Power	15
It Is Natural	17
I Let Go	19
I Call Upon	23
My Word So Strong	25
Resolute	27
Mini Prayers	29
Conclusion	34

Introduction

Prayer is a powerful way in which to contact our innate powers. Traditionally, prayer is thought of as asking God, or a Higher Power, for help. In this series of books, prayer is proclaiming who you are and stating it as fact. It is reclaiming your birthright as a powerful being who is meant to receive all that it desires. (Please keep in mind that these prayers are not from the Bible and are non-traditional in nature.)

Prayers for Everyone™ is a series of themed books that consist of ten prayers each. Strength (Book 1) is the first book in the series and focuses on assisting you in harnessing your inner strength. The prayers that follow will remind you of how strong you are both mentally and spiritually. They will remind you of the powerful force that lies within you and is at your disposal in every moment. Reciting these prayers often will bring out the stronger you. We can never overstate who we are. The more we pray the more powerful we become in that prayer.

Utilize these prayers to empower yourself in every moment; before you leave in the morning, throughout your day and in the evening. Read each prayer with conviction and with knowing even though you may not, as of yet, truly know. Eventually, you will know. Read them slowly and pause often so as to absorb what they are speaking to you. There is no rush.

Relax and breathe.

Recite your prayers both in the good times and the not so good times and begin to memorize them. When you make it a habit to reach for a prayer in the difficult times and in the joyful times, you will become more conscious of when you are spiraling into a not so pleasant space. As you become more adept at being conscious, your prayer will enter your mind on its own. It will become automatic and you will then find yourself consistently in a more powerful state of being.

Use these prayers often, especially during your travel times from home to work or wherever you might be headed (not while driving, of course). Your time is valuable. Use it wisely by reaffirming to yourself and reminding yourself of who you are and the power you hold.

I recommend, for quick access to your strength, that you extract your favorite verse from any of the prayers and repeat it throughout the day, or when you find yourself in a challenging situation. Short and powerful phrases from the prayers that resonate with you the most will establish themselves quicker and easier in your mind; we call these *Mini Prayers* and have included them at the end of the book. Feel free to choose the verse that feels most powerful to you.

Most importantly, this is fun. Prayer is not meant to be

too serious. Enjoy yourself. Enjoy remembering who you are. Enjoy becoming the powerful being that you are. Enjoy being you!

◇

Definitions

PRAYER is reaffirming who you are. It is reminding yourself of how powerful you are, where you come from, what you're made of and who you are. The more you pray the more you remember and unleash your powers. Other words that might be used in place of the word prayer are meditation, affirmations, focus, quiet time etc.

GOD is equivalent to Consciousness, Spirit, Higher Power, Infinite Intelligence, Higher Self, Source, Energy, Wiser Self, The Divine, Intuition etc.

I is you. When you are reading these prayers embrace them as your own. Read them from your point of view.

YOU is God.

Nicole Rivera

I PRAY

Today, I pray
That my word
Be one
With your word.

Let it be spoken
With plenty on its tongue
And with compassion
And knowing
In its heart.

Let it be filled
With the power
And the knowing
That you embody.

Let my word be spoken
With faith
And with trust
In you,
So that all good
May come to pass.

I rest in peace
Knowing
All is fulfilled.

Nicole Rivera

Infused

I am infused
With your words
Of strength.

I speak my power.
I know my truth.

I am complete.

Nicole Rivera

10

EMBODIMENT

I am the embodiment of all:
Wisdom,
Plenty,
Well-being.

I am the beginning
That has no end.

I am the light
That seizes the night.

I am the fulfillment
Of all
That surrounds me.

I am full.
I am whole.
I am complete.

I am.

Nicole Rivera

I Am Strength

I am strength
Unto myself.
I am all I need
To be
Who I am.

I am full
Unto myself.
I am provided for
By that
Which I am.

I am the well-being
That I desire.
I am all life-giving
And joy.

I AM THAT POWER

I am that power
That flows in,
Around
And through
All there is.

I am that power
That comes forth
From the unknown
To discover and play.

I am that power
That compels a tree to grow,
A bird to fly,
A fish to swim,
A lion to roar.

I am that power
That commands the ocean
To spread across the land,
The fire to spew forth
From the volcano,
The wind to howl.

I am that power
That breathes life
Into the living
And awakens the dead.

I am that power…

15

*

IT IS NATURAL

It is natural to be
Plentiful.

It is natural to be
Full.

It is natural to experience
Well-being.

It is natural to be
Joyful.

It is natural to experience
Laughter.

It is natural to be
Beautiful.

It is natural to be
Ageless.

It is natural to be
Whole.

It is natural to be
God.

Nicole Rivera

I LET GO

I let go...
I breathe…
I relax…

I let go
And I trust
The invisible world
Where desires
Are fulfilled
And all is complete.

I let go
And I trust
In the power
That is me,

Though I cannot
See nor touch
This beautiful thing.

I let go
And I trust
In the love
That creates
All there is,

con't

Nicole Rivera

A love so deep
It anxiously awaits
My recognition of it;
To embrace it
As my own.

I let go
And let God do
What I could not do
With an army of men.

I let go
And let God
Proclaim to me,
"All is well.
All is love."

I let go…
I breathe…
I relax…

As I watch
My life unfold
And God create
So perfectly,
Trusting
In that power
That I have been reminded of
Once more,
The power of me.

Nicole Rivera

Ω

I Call Upon

I call upon
My strength.
I raise my head!

I call upon
My courage.
I stand tall!

I call upon
My wisdom.
I look straight ahead!

I call upon
My power.
I speak my word!

I am all there is.
I am the strength of all the ages.
I am the courage of the many.
I am the wisdom of the ancients.
I am the power that rules over all that exists.

I am unstoppable!
I am unbeatable!
I am victorious!
I am God!

A

MY WORD SO STRONG

I let go
And let God heal
As I pray
My powerful word.

A word so strong
It moves mountains,
Raises the sun,
Stirs the wind,
Calms the waters.

A word so strong
It brightens the night,
Restores the sick,
Arouses the dead.

A word so strong,
A word so powerful,
It destroys all
Unlike itself.

My word so strong...

∞

Resolute

I am resolute in harnessing my power within,
Steadfast in seeking joy,
Dogged in my exhibition of well-being,
Unshakable in my expression of plenty,
Determined in my quest for the truth,
Destined to be me.
I am complete.

Nicole Rivera

♠

Mini Prayers

On the following pages you will find what we call *Mini Prayers* – excerpts from each prayer. They are an excellent way to keep yourself uplifted throughout the day if you have not, as of yet, committed the full prayer to memory. They are also very useful in the event you need immediate relief. Because they are short, they are easy to remember. Please feel free to extract the parts of the prayers that resonate with you the most and enjoy.

I Pray

Today, I pray
That my word
Be one
With your word.

Infused

I speak my power.
I know my truth.

Embodiment

I am full.
I am whole.
I am complete.

I Am Strength

I am the well-being
That I desire.
I am all life-giving
And joy.

♣

I Am That Power

I am that power
That comes forth
From the unknown
To discover and play.

⁙

It Is Natural

It is natural to be
God.

✳

Nicole Rivera

I Let Go

I let go
And let God
Proclaim to me,
"All is well.
All is love."

❦

I Call Upon

I am unstoppable!
I am unbeatable!
I am victorious!
I am God!

Ω

My Word So Strong

I let go
And let God heal
As I pray
My powerful word.

A

RESOLUTE

I am steadfast
In seeking joy.

∞

CONCLUSION

Thank you for reading through these powerful prayers that, when read consistently and embodied fully, will assist you in remembering and living who you are.

Remember to use these prayers as a tool to assist you in relieving yourself of the not so nice thoughts that press upon you throughout the day. Know that there is a more powerful word beneath it that awaits to break through. You are the only one that can help it escape by changing your thoughts. Slowly, but with certainty, through the repetition and embodiment of these prayers, the more powerful word will take over and relieve you. It will remind you of your greatness and the love and power that you inherently are. Most of all, relax. There is no need to rush; there is only calm and knowing. Read each prayer focusing on each word; get lost in them and breathe. The truth is being revealed to you. Let it in.

My intention is that you will walk throughout your day feeling empowered, encouraged, and enlightened. All of these attributes are you.

Thank you and may all of your desires be fulfilled in this bountiful day.

Nicole

For other prayer books please visit:
http://www.nicolerivera.com.

If you would like to book Nicole to speak at your event please email cs@isaiahpublications.com.

Thank you!

www.ingramcontent.com/pod-product-compliance
Lightning Source LLC
Chambersburg PA
CBHW060633030426
42337CB00018B/3341